APPLE WATCH SE

Quick And Easy Guide To Unlo ... rour
Apple Watch Like A Pro

Daniel McDermott

Contents

Introduction

If you're the owner of an Apple Watch, or wondering what exactly Apple's so-called iWatch actually does, you have one of the best smartwatches in the world at your disposal.

But there's a steep learning curve – and getting the most from your Apple Watch and its bevy of fitness, workout and time-saving features is key.

That's what this ultimate guide to the Apple Watch sets out to achieve. We've covered everything from the basic questions, to really ramping you up as a power user – covering top tips, essential apps and stylish ways to make your smartwatch even better.

Getting Started: How to set up and pair your Apple Watch with your iPhone

The Apple Watch and iPhone may be two distinct pieces of hardware, but one can't exist without the other. When you buy a new Apple Watch, turning it on is only the first step – next comes pairing it with an iPhone. When it is time for you to pair your Apple Watch with your iPhone, you will need to use the Apple Watch app for iOS. You should be able to find it pre-installed on your iPhone or via the App Store if you have removed it previously.

There are various ways to pair your Apple Watch to your iPhone, depending what makes the most sense for your needs. You can choose to automatically pair your watch to your iPhone or do it manually. For automatically pairing, follow these steps:

- Launch the Watch app on your iPhone. (you can also bring your Apple Watch near your iPhone to bring up a similar interface to the Airpods pairing screen, which will then launch the Watch app).

- Tap Start Pairing.

- Move your phone over your Apple Watch until your Apple Watch is lined up in the center of the yellow rectangle. Then when you see a message that says "your apple watch is paired," you will know that you have completed the step successfully.

- Choose whether to set up your Apple Watch from scratch or to restore Apple watch from a backup.

That is how to pair your device automatically. However, if you can't get the Apple Watch to start the pairing process automatically, you can manually pair your iPhone and Watch. Instead of using the nifty QR-code-style process, you will use your Apple Watch's name to start the pairing process.

- Launch the Watch app on your iPhone. (you can also bring your Apple Watch near your iPhone to bring up a similar interface to the Airpods pairing screen, which will then launch the Watch app).
- Tap the Start Pairing

- Tap Pair Apple Watch Manually

- On your Apple Watch, tap *i* to view the device's name.

- On your iPhone, select your Apple Watch from the list.

- Finally, choose whether to set up your Apple Watch from scratch or to restore Apple Watch from a backup.

Setting up Apple Watch From Scratch

If this is your first Apple Watch or you simply don't want to carry over old data, it is very simple to set up your smartwatch from scratch

- Once you have finished the pairing process, tap **Set Up as New Apple Watch.**

- Tap either **Left** or **Right** to tell Apple Watch on which wrist you plan to wear it.

- Tap **Agree** to accept the watchOS terms and conditions. Then Tap **Agree** again to confirm.

- Set up **Activation Lock** and **Find My iPhone** by entering your Apple ID.

- Tap **OK** to indicate you understand **Shared Settings** for iPhone and Apple Watch.

- Tap **Create a Passcode** to create a passcode for Apple Watch.

  - Tap **Add a Long Passcode** to add a passcode longer than four digits.

  - Tap **Don't Add Passcode** if you'd rather not have a passcode on your Apple Watch.

- On your Apple Watch, tap to create a four-digit passcode. Then enter your passcode once more to confirm

- If you have an Apple Watch series 3 with LTE service, choose whether to **Set Up Cellular** on your Apple Watch

- Set up Apple Pay or you can set it up later. You may need to enter your card security code to the entire number, depending on which card you are adding.

- On your iPhone, tap **Continue** to indicate you understand **Emergency SOS.**
- Tap **Install All** to install all of the available watch apps on your iPhone (watchOS apps are included with iOS apps).
  - Tap **Choose Later** if you'd rather not install all of the available watchOS apps on your iPhone.
- Finally, allow your Apple Watch to **sync with your iPhone**. When it is finished syncing, then your Watch is ready to roll.

How to change your Apple Watch face

With just a swipe, you can change your Apple Watch from chronograph to color, modular to utility, Mickey or Minnie Mouse to simple, motion to solar, astronomy to... you get the idea. Each has a different density and character, a different capacity for complication and customization. Best of all, changing your watch face is really easy to do once you know how!

Changing a watch face is easier than ever. It takes a little practice, but once you get the hang of it, you'll want to change your watch face every time you change your clothes.

- Navigate to the watch face on your Apple Watch by pressing the **Digital Crown**.
- Swipe left or right to cycle through available watch faces

Note: The key to switching faces when swiping is to start from the very edge of the screen. Actually start from off the edge of the screen to ensure you are far enough over.

How to add an Apple Watch face to your list

You can add any number of different styles to the list of watch faces you can switch between.

- Open the Watch app on your iPhone.
- Tap the Face Gallery tab.

- Tap a watch face from the list to select it. They are organized by type.
- Tap Add.

The new watch face will automatically be added to your Apple Watch as the current display.

How to remove an Apple Watch face from

your list via your iPhone

If your list of watch faces is getting too long, you can remove ones you don't use.

- Open the Watch app on your iPhone.
- Tap the My Watch tab.
- Under My Faces, tap Edit.

- Tap the red remove button (-) on the left side of a face.
- Tap Remove on the right side of the face to remove it from your list.

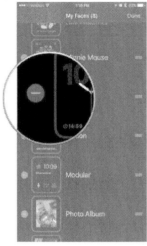 

- The watch face will automatically be removed from your Apple Watch.

How to remove a watch face via your Apple Watch

You can remove a watch face from your list right on your Apple Watch.

- Navigate to the watch face on your Apple Watch by pressing the Digital Crown.
- Press firmly on the watch face to open the customize menu.
- Swipe left or right to select a watch face. Swipe up on the watch face you want to

11

remove.

- Tap   Remove

How to organize your list of Apple Watch faces

You can order your watch faces so that specific ones are next to each other, or listed by color, or how every you want them to be organized.

- Open the Watch app on your iPhone.
- Tap the My Watch tab.
- Under My Faces, tap Edit.
- Press and hold the organize icon on the right side of the watch face. It looks like three lines (≡).
- Drag the watch face to its new position on your list.

The new order of watch faces will automatically appear on your Apple Watch.

How To Use The Digital Crown And Side Button

In some ways, the iPhone X takes after the Apple Watch's design: Both have no home button, both are all screen, and both have a surprising amount of functionality for having relatively few physical buttons. The Apple Watch like the iPhone X, has a side button, which you use to turn it on and off along with a variety of other tricks and tasks. But it also has an interface uniquely Apple Watch: The Digital Crown.

The only traditional button on the watch, the side button not only powers and turns off the watch, but controls the Dock and emergency features. If your Apple Watch is on, you can press and hold the side button to access the power screen, then slide the Power Off slider to turn the watch off.

The Apple watch medical ID and SOS features are hidden behind the power screen, which you access by pressing and holding the side button. Swipe either Medical ID or SOS to activate either feature. Note: Swiping SOS will place a call to the local authorities and is only meant to be used in an emergency.

Using The Kaleidoscope Watch Face On Your Apple Watch

Watch OS 4 brings a bunch of awesome changes

to your Apple Watch, including a new Kaleidoscope watch face. Or, if you want to be technical: watch face(s), as there are multiple permutations of the Kaleidoscope pattern. Each looks cool and colorful. Apple offers eight default Kaleidoscope options, but you can also make your own from any photo on your iPhone.

There are two ways you can create a new watch face: through the Apple watch app on your iPhone, or through the Apple watch itself. From the watch app:

- Launch the watch app from your Home screen
- Tap the Face Gallery tab.
- Tap Kaleidoscape.
- Tap the Photo you want to use.

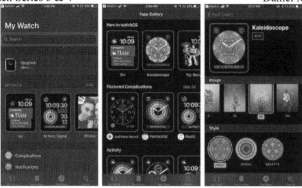

- Tap the style you desire.
- Choose the Complications you want on the watch face.
- Tap Add.

From the Apple Watch:

- Navigate to your current watch face on your Apple watch.
- Press firmly on the watch face
- Scroll all the way to the right
- Tap on New
- Scroll until you the Kaleidoscope option
- Tap on the Kaleidoscope face.

 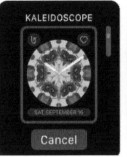 

- Press firmly on the watch face to enter edit mode
- Press Customize
- Choose which preset photo you'd like to use.
- Choose your Kaleidoscope style.
- Choose your Complications
- Press the digital crown to finish.

You can make a custom Kaleidoscope watch face by launching the watch app from your Home screen. Then tap the Face Gallery and choose Kaleidoscope. Tap custom photo and choose the photo you want to use. Tap the Style you want to use. Either you select Facet or Radial. Choose the Complications you want on the watch face and tap add.

Basics Of The Apple Watch

When the apple watch is completely powered off, to turn the apple watch on, you need only to press and hold the side button to see the apple logo which will inform you the apple watch is turning on. If You want to power off the Apple watch completely, you need only to press and hold the side button, followed by sliding the *Power Off* toggle.

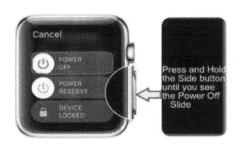

If you want to turn on your Apple watch when it is asleep, all you need to do is bring it up close to your face, or if that doesn't work, you can also tap to wake up the apple watch. Then to put the apple watch to sleep, you need only to drop your wrist down, and it will turn off.

Let us talk about some of the different components of the apple watch. We have the display in the front, and there is also the apple watch digital crown by the side. This digital crown allows you to scroll and zoom in using the little slider on the side. It acts similarly to a regular watch knob. In addition to that, there is a home button that you can press. This acts as the normal home button that you might have used on your iPhone. Here is how it works, by pressing the front of the home button; it will allow you to go to the main area where you will see all of the different app icons display on the screen. You can also press it back again to enter back into the clock face.

A single tap will enter you in and out of your application view and your clock face. A double tap will send you to the previous application that was open. You can press and hold to activate Siri. The side button also does some very important things on your Apple watch. One press of the side button will bring up your favorites; you can scroll through them to contact them individually. Let us say you have a favorite that you wanted to contact, press on them and you can give them a call, message or your heartbeat or other pictures if they have an apple watch as well.

You can also double tap the side button to access Apple pay. Pressing and holding the button will bring up the menu that will allow you to power off your device. One more thing for you to know is that the Apple watch doesn't just respond to regular touches and taps, it also responds to something called force touch, which is when you press and hold more firmly on the screen. This allows you to access a whole different settings menu. In conclusion, you have a speaker, microphone, and the heart rate sensor which will monitor your heart rate while you are doing exercises. You can also take off the bands using the little button at the top and bottom − press in on the little button and pull the band out from side to side. To put the bands back, slide it in, and it will lock into place.

Features And Settings

We will now look at some important features and settings of the Apple Watch. You can access the Apple Watch home screen just by pressing once on the digital crown. You can then move around the home screen by pressing and holding your finger to wipe around, and you will see the different applications that are available. Tap on any application to open it up.

You can rearrange your tap icon by pressing and holding on one of the app icons and moving it around until you find a position that suits you better and then release your hand. You can more easily access the home screen of your watch by going into the "my watch application" on your phone, clicking on app play out and pressing and holding the app icons and moving it to the position you desire. Once you do that through your phone, it will automatically change the app display on your watch.

If you want to adjust the brightness and settings, go the settings application and scroll down to brightness and text size, and this will allow you to increase the brightness (there are three different notches) or decrease the brightness. I like to keep mine on the medium settings. You can also change the text size and also add bold text which is a cool feature if you want something a little bit easier to read.

Through the settings, you can also adjust the sound (loud and soft) and haptics. You can also mute the device, and it will only tap you when it receives a notification. You can scroll down to see the haptics and select the kind of tap you like on your wrist.

If you want to access the Do Not Disturb, Airplane Mode, Mute, and Ping your iPhone, all you have to do is to swipe up and then scroll to the left until you see the connected tab. This is going to allow you to turn on/of the Do Not Disturb, which make sure you receive or don't receive notifications on your Apple watch. You can also turn on/off the airplane mode, and sound. You can also ping your iPhone If you lose your iPhone and you don't know where it is, and it will instantly ping your iPhone.

From the same glances menu which is the list of different quick view applications, you can swipe over to see your current battery life, and it will be displayed in percentage. There is another cool thing I love which is called the Power Reserve. This is great for reserving your battery when the battery is low. When it is on power reserve, it will continue to display the time, but all of the other apps will not be available to use. To access this mode, all you have to do is to press and hold on the side button, then swipe to enter power reserve. But please do know that your watch will only display the time when on power reserve, you cannot access any other thing including the side button. The only way to get back everything is to restart your Apple Watch completely.

Notifications

If you have a red dot at the top of your Apple Watch screen, that means that you have unread notifications. If you had instantly gotten those notifications, you would be able to see them on the screen within about a minute of receiving them. However, if you wait for a certain period, a red dot will appear. All you have to do is swipe downward so that you can read all the different messages that you just received. Click on the message to read, and you can either dismiss or reply the message.

When you click on reply, it will come up with quick and easy responses based on what it thinks that the text is saying. You can choose to accept those responses or send your text. You can also send a smiley face or dictate text for Siri to send for you. It is that simple! Please know that email also shows up in the notification section as well.

Glances

Let me show a little bit more of all the different

glances that you can access. The first glance that you have is the one that allows you to turn on your "airplane," and "do not disturb." You can also swipe over to access the music settings, which allows you to play, pause, go forward or backward on your music. You can also increase and decrease the volume; you can play music that is on your iPhone or music saved locally to your Apple Watch.

The next glance you will see when you swipe over again is your heart rate, followed by the activity app, events, weather, stocks, maps, world times, etc. Those are the different glances that we have.

Messages

If you want to use messages on the Apple watch, tap on the messages icon, and you will see your most recent messages. You can decide to tap on it to see the conversation.

If you want to reply, kindly scroll down to click Reply and send another message. You can also send some different emojis that you would like. You can send your message as either text or audio. Now, if you want to send a new message, just press and hold using force touch. Then click "new message." Choose your contact, create the message and then send it. That is how to use messages on your Apple Watch.

Email

Email on the Apple watch is a breeze, click on the mail application on the apps menu. You can click on an email to read it and read a brief blurb of your email. Unfortunately, you do need to reply to the emails using your phone. However, there is a cool feature available, if you have your email open on your Apple Watch, you will go to your phone and in the bottom left-hand corner, swipe up, input your passcode, and you will be brought directly to that email. This is called hands-off, and it is a great feature available on the Apple Watch.

Answering Phone Calls

Handling call in the Apple Watch is very easy to do. When you get a call that comes into your Apple Watch, you will be able to see who is calling; you can accept the call, deny the call or scroll down to send a message. You can also answer on your iPhone. Once you click answer on your iPhone, it will hit hold, and you can then answer it directly on your iPhone. The Apple Watch is great at allowing you to quickly answer phone calls, especially when you are out about a run, or in an area where it is a little bit difficult to whip out your phone.

Calendars & Reminders

The Apple Watch makes keeping track of your events amazing. If you go into the main home screen, you can scroll over to the calendar section. This will show you all of the different events that you have for any given day. Another cool feature is that you can include your calendar directly on your watch itself by pressing and holding the screen, then select customizing and choose the calendar option using a digital crown. Just like you set reminders on your iPhone, iPad, or iPod touch, you can activate Siri on your Apple Watch and say something like "At 7 pm, remind me to call Dad." It doesn't make a calendar entry for this event, but you are reminded with a sound, a vibration on your wrist, and a text. Remember, Apple Watch doesn't use the keyboard, so you must dictate the reminder.

To add a new event, press and hold the Apple Watch screen while inside the Calendar app. You are prompted to tap New and then select Date and Time for the event, and you can speak into your wrist for the title of your event. Don't also forget that Apple Watch pulls calendar events from your iPhone. You don't always have to manually check your calendar for upcoming appointments, as you should receive a notification about it (and feel a slight pulse). Some users like to be reminded an hour before an event, for instance, while others might only want a five-minute reminder. This is all handled in your iPhone calendar app.

Also, when you receive calendar invitations, you can accept or decline immediately and even email the organizer using preset responses. You can follow the steps to accept or decline a calendar invitation or to reply to the organizer from your Apple Watch:

- When you receive a calendar invite via email or message, you should receive a notification with the proposed meeting date, time and information. This is where you have the chance to act on it, and you won't have to reach for your iPhone.

- Use your finger to swipe down on the notification or twist the Digital Crown button and then you can tap Accept, Maybe, or Decline. You can't suggest an alternate date or time or anything – as you can do with some email programs – but this lets the organizer receive some response.

- Swipe up to respond to an invitation and firmly press (Digital Touch) the display while you are looking at the event details and choose to call the organizer or send a voice message recording. All these functions can also be performed in the calendar app – instead of via notification – by tapping on the meeting details and choosing to accept, decline, or reply.

Don't also forget that you can raise your wrist and say "Hey, Siri" or press and hold the Digital Crown button and then say something like "Add calendar entry, pharmacist appointment, for 11 a.m. tomorrow." This spoken text is added to your calendar and synced with your iPhone too. You can also use Siri to ask Apple Watch about upcoming events, such as "What is on my calendar today?" "When is my appointment at the pharmacist?"

You don't need your iPhone to receive calendar alerts on your Apple Watch. Therefore, if you go on a run or accidentally leave your iPhone at the office, you can still see existing calendar entries, but you can't add one. Why? Because Apple Watch doesn't have a keyboard, you have to use Siri to dictate new appointments, which is not possible without the iPhone.

How to Add & Listen to Music on Your Apple Watch

You probably already know that you can control your iPhone's music from the Apple Watch. And if you have the Apple Watch Series 3 or 4, you know you can stream music directly on your watch without your iPhone. But if you have an Apple Watch without cellular data and want to leave your phone at home, how will you listen to music without your iPhone? And if you have the Apple Watch Series 3 with Cellular, how can you listen to music without data or Wi-Fi? The best way to listen to music while running or doing another iPhone-free activity is to put it on your Apple Watch, of course.

We'll go over how to make a playlist on your iPhone, how to sync music to your Apple Watch, and how to pair Bluetooth headphones with your Apple Watch so you can listen without data. Here's everything you need to know about how to add music to your Apple Watch.

If you use Apple Music, make sure the songs you want on your Apple Watch are downloaded to your iPhone before attempting to sync music.

Since watchOS 4.1, you can now have more than one playlist on your Apple Watch at a time, as long as you have a Series 1 or later.

How to Make a Playlist on iPhone

- On your iPhone, open the Music app.
- Tap My Music. Then tap Playlists at the top.
- Select New Playlist.
- Add all the songs you want on your Apple Watch to the playlist.
- You can always add more songs later as well.
- Tap Done.

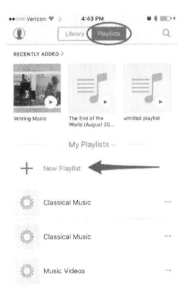

How to Sync Music to Apple Watch

- Place your Apple Watch on the charger.

- On your iPhone, make sure Bluetooth is turned on. You can swipe up for Control Center and see this at a glance.

- Open the Watch app on iPhone.

- Choose Music.

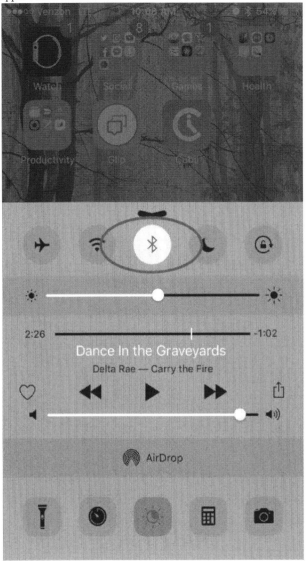

- Tap Synced Playlist.
- Find and select the Playlist you want to sync onto your Apple Watch.

- If your Apple Watch is not charging, it will remain as Sync Pending until your watch is within range and charging. Then it will automatically begin to sync.

- Once the Sync is complete, your playlist is officially available to play from Apple Watch without your iPhone.

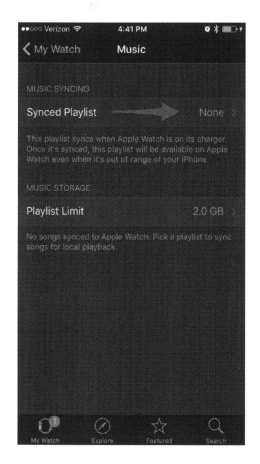

How to Pair Bluetooth Headphones with Apple Watch

The next step is to pair your Bluetooth headphones with your Apple Watch. Since there's no headphone jack on Apple Watch, you will have to use Bluetooth headphones or earbuds. To do this:

- Turn on your headphones and put them in pairing mode, usually represented by a blue blinking light.
- On your Apple Watch, open Settings.
- Tap Bluetooth.
- Select your headphones under Devices.

How to Listen to Your Playlist on Apple Watch

Once your playlist has synced to your Apple Watch and your headphones are paired with your watch, you can listen to the playlist on your Apple Watch without your iPhone. To listen:

- On your Apple Watch, open the Music app.
- At the top it will say, Choose a music source to play from. Tap the watch icon. If you don't see this, you can access it by hard pressing the screen, selecting source, and choosing Apple Watch.
- Select Playlists.

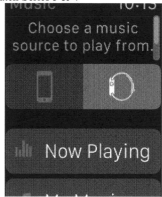 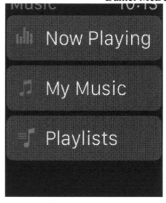

- At the top you'll see, On My Apple Watch. Select the playlist, press play and your music will begin!

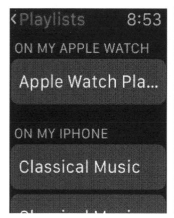 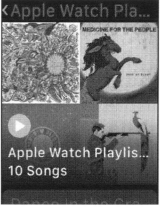

If for some reason you haven't already paired Bluetooth headphones with the Apple Watch, it will prompt you to do so before playing the music.

How To Set Up And Use Activity Sharing On Apple Watch

If you like to workout with friends or find a little healthy competition between you and someone else important to achieving your fitness goals, the Activity app can help you out. When you enable Sharing on your iPhone and Apple Watch, other people can view your progress, compare and challenge themselves to work out as hard or harder than you, and even send you taunting messages along the way.

What activity data can be shared when you connect with friends? When you add a pal to your sharing screen, you will see all their Activity data from that day forward – and they will get all of yours, too. Your activity data is broken down into a few categories:

- Your day's Activity rings (Move, Exercise, and Stand) and your personal goals for each

- Calories Burned

- Minutes exercised

- Hours stood

- Steps taken

- Distance traveled

Your Apple Watch and the Activity app will never share more personal and confidential data with your friends, like your heartbeat, or any other Health data potentially collected by the watch. The following steps will teach you how you can turn on activity sharing:

- Launch the Activity app from your iPhone's home screen

- Tap the Sharing button

- Tap the red plus sign (+) in the upper right corner

- Type the name or Apple ID of the friend you would like to share your activity progress with
- Tap Send

Once that is done, you will be able to view your progress alongside that of your friends inside the Sharing pane of the Activity app.

You can also share your activity rings without using activity sharing. If you want to brag to someone who doesn't have an Apple Watch, you can share your activity rings as a stand-alone image from the sharing screen. Here's how.

- From the sharing screen, tap on the Me entry.
- Tap on the Share button in the upper right corner.
- Tap Save Image, Copy, Message, Mail, or any other share sheet option.

Let us now look at how you can view your friends' shared activity data. After you have added a few friends to your sharing screen, you will see their Activity rings show up alongside their name, and (by default) their move goal percentage and calories burned.

If you are less about calories and more interested in exercise time or miles walked, you can tap the Sort button in the upper left corner to change metrics: you can sort by alphabetical name, Move goal, Exercise goal, Steps goal, or Number of Workouts.

How to Take An ECG (Electrocardiogram) On Apple Watch

For now, Apple has made taking an ECG (electrocardiogram) on Apple Watch Series 4 available to users in the US. It appears Apple isn't allowing the feature to be used outside the US by adjusting region settings.

Before getting started, Apple notes that for accurate readings, you'll need to be wearing your Apple Watch on the wrist that is selected in settings.

Initial set up:

- Make sure your Apple Watch Series 4 is updated to watchOS 5.1.2 and iPhone is updated to iOS 12.1.1
- Open the **Watch app** on iPhone and tap **Heart**

- Tap **Set up the ECG app in Health** and follow the prompts

- The ECG app will now be functional on your Apple Watch

- Tap the **ECG app** (white icon with red heartbeat waveform)

- Make sure your Apple Watch is **snug on your wrist**

- With your arms relaxed on your lap or tabletop, **hold the Digital Crown with your finger** for 30 seconds (don't depress the button)

- Keep your finger in place until the countdown is finished.

Here is a screenshot of how the process looks:

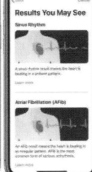
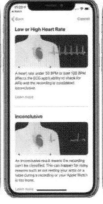

Daniel McDermott

48

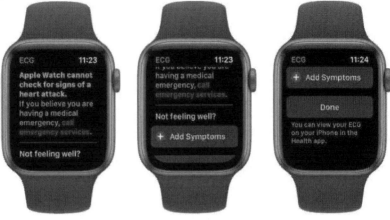

Keep in mind the limits of Apple Watch's health features:

- It cannot detect a heart attack
- It cannot detect a blood clot or stroke
- It cannot detect other heart defects

How to Use Siri On Your Apple Watch

With Apple Watch, you can ask Siri to answer questions, perform tasks, and provide information. Siri is especially helpful on the watch as you can issue commands by voice instead of tapping tiny buttons. Siri is a fixture of your Apple Watch, no matter which edition you own. But with the Apple Watch series 3, Siri can answer your requests by text or by voice and talk to you over a paired Bluetooth headset. Siri can also tie in with your iPhone to control your music. Let us see how you can use Siri on the Apple Watch.

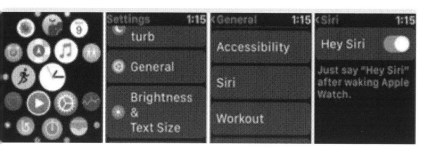

1. Enable "Hey Siri"

You can activate Siri by holding down the Digital

crown until you see the "What can I help you with?" screen. But you may also want to activate Siri by voice. To enable this, tap the Digital Crown to move to the Home Screen. Tap on Settings>General>Siri. Then make sure "Hey Siri" is turned on. Press the Digital Crown again to jump back to your watch face.

2. Siri Awaits Your Command

With an Apple Watch Series 1 or 2, Siri can only display its responses in text on the screen. But with an Apple Watch Series 3, Siri can talk back at you. To set this up on a Series 3 watch, tap on Settings > General > Siri. Then choose one of the following three options: Always On, Control with Silent Mode, or Headphones Only. If your iPhone is not nearby or doesn't have "Hey Siri" activated, or you are in a quiet room, you can talk to your watch without having to raise your wrist and say those magic words: "Hey Siri." Your watch face should display your words while Siri awaits your command.

The commands, questions, and requests you can issue to Siri are too numerous to detail here. You will find a list of the many things you can ask Siri at Apple's Siri webpage. You can also ask Siri "What can I ask you," and Siri will display all the different things that you ask. However, let us look at some examples.

Ask Siri "what will the temperature be tomorrow?" The Apple Watch Series 1 or 2 will display the temperature forecast for tomorrow. With a Series 3, Siri speaks the temperature forecast.

3. Ask Siri

You can also ask Siri the following, "Hey Siri, open the Photos app," "Hey Siri, start an Outdoor Walk," "Hey Siri, call Dad on mobile," "Hey Siri, show me my appointments for the week," "Hey Siri, show me nearby Mexican restaurants," and Siri will answer you accordingly. Playing music is another skill Siri offers on the Apple Watch.

4. Music

Ask Siri to play a song, album, or artist from your Apple Music or iCloud music collection, and you can listen over a paired Bluetooth speaker or headset.

You can also use Siri to control music playing on your iPhone. Rev up a song or album on your iPhone, either manually or by telling Siri to play it. For example, "Hey Siri, play Sgt. Pepper's Lonely Hearts Club Band." The music starts playing on your iPhone. But if you glance at your Apple Watch, you will see a mini player where you can pause, play, skip ahead, skip back, and change the volume.

Finally, you can change your watch face to a dedicated Siri face, which is available with watchOS 4 or higher. To grab the new face, open the Watch app on your iPhone. Tap on the Face Gallery icon at the bottom of the screen. The top of the Face Gallery screen displays the newest available watch faces, including the Siri's face. Tap on the Siri's face to download it and then tap on the Add button. Tap on the My Watch icon at the bottom of the screen. Swipe to the end of the list of watch faces, and you will see the new Siri face.

You can then swipe each face on your Apple Watch until you come to the Siri's face. To talk to Siri, tap on the Siri button on the face. Pose your question, request, or command to Siri, and the voice assistant will comply.

How to Browse   the Internet on Apple Watch

Through watchOS 5's WebKit Integration

With watchOS 5, Apple has added support for WebKit, which is designed to allow you to view content from the web right on your wrist, something that's entirely new to the Apple Watch.

There's no full web browser so you're not going to see a Safari app for Apple Watch anytime soon, but you can now click on and open web links in apps like Mail and Messages.

WebKit in Messages

If someone sends you a link to your Apple Watch in the Messages app, you can tap on it to open up a little mini web browser right in the Messages app.

You can open all kinds of webpages, from restaurant menus to airline flight information. Webpages are interactive and you can click on links and browse as you normally would.

WebKit in Mail

Just like Messages, if you get an email with a web link in it, you can open it up using the Mail app. You can also view HTML emails on the Apple Watch for the first time thanks to the WebKit integration.

Using Google and Other Websites on Apple Watch

As we mentioned earlier, there's no built-in Safari app on the Apple Watch for browsing the web, but you can cheat. Here's how:

- From your iPhone or Mac, send yourself an iMessage with a link to Google.com (or any other search engine).

- On the Apple Watch, open up the Messages app.

- Tap on your name, and then tap on the Google.com link that you sent yourself.
- Wait for the Google site to load on the Apple Watch.
- Tap on the search field.
- Speak or spell out whatever you want to search for.
- Tap the search button.

You can load all kinds of websites on the Apple Watch, from Wikipedia to restaurant sites for finding menus, to airline check-in sites to websites like MacRumors.com. It's essentially a full browser that's been miniaturized for the wrist.

Some content will not load on the Apple Watch. You can't watch YouTube videos, for example, nor will other types of video content load. Complicated websites with a lot of content, such as news sites, can take awhile to load or can refuse to load all together, so simple browsing is best on the Apple Watch.

Where possible, the little Apple Watch browser will use Reader Mode for text heavy websites, so you will see simple, easy-to-view sites with no ads. Mobile optimized sites work the best on the Apple Watch.

Using Google in the Messages app for browsing the web isn't something that you're going to want to do all the time because it's slow and tedious on such a small screen, not to mention it eats up a lot of battery, but it's useful for an emergency where you need to look something up and don't have an iPhone handy.

For browsing the web on the Apple Watch, you will always need to use the search cheat because Apple doesn't allow access to the URL bar. You can tap it, but there's no way to enter a web address.

WebKit Gestures

WebKit on Apple Watch supports several gestures, which are outlined below.

- Use the Digital Crown or a finger on the screen to scroll.

- Double tap to zoom in and double tap again to zoom out.

- Long press to access options for Back, Forward, Reload, and Reader Mode.

- Swipe to move forwards or backwards through different sites.

- Tap a text field to speak or spell out text.

How to Clear Website Data on Apple Watch

Being able to browse the web on the Apple Watch through Mail and Messages means that your Apple Watch is storing some website data. You can delete all of this data in the Settings app. Here's how:

- Open the Settings app on Apple Watch.

- Choose General.
- Scroll down to Website Data.
- Select "Clear Website Data."

Using this option will remove all website cookies, credentials, and browsing data. It does not appear that Apple Watch stores any browsing history in a viewable format, so there's no option to clear just history.

Availability

According to Apple, WebKit integration is limited to Apple Watch Series 3 models. WebKit and websites will not load on the Apple Watch Series 1 and Series 2 models.

How to Use And Personalize Your Apple Watch

The Apple Watch may not have become as indispensable as your smartphone. But since Apple first took the wraps off its smartwatch in 2015, the Apple Watch has still managed to fill a need for many users, and the addition of cellular connectivity in the latest version makes this gadget even more useful. The key to making the Apple Watch an essential part of your life? Know how to get the most of it. We've got an in-depth guide to Apple's smartwatch, but let's start with some quick tips and tricks that make the Apple Watch even easier to use.

Switching Between Apps

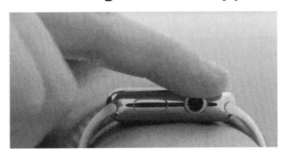

To jump back to your most recently used app, double-tap the Digital Crown.

Switching Watch Faces

You might want to set up multiple watch faces for multiple purposes — one with a minimal face for those times when you don't want a cluttered interface, the other with a more fun display. To switch back and forth, you can simply swipe to the left and right from the watch face.

Rearranging Applications in the Dock

WatchOS 4 overhauled the Dock, which gives you easy access to your most frequently used apps. But what if you want to change the order in which those apps appear?

- Open the Watch app on your iPhone and select Dock.
- Choose whether you want your Dock

ordered by recently used apps or favorites.

- Tap Edit to choose your favorite apps. You can add up to 10 apps to your Dock, which is accessible by pressing the side button on the watch.

Muting an Incoming Call

When a call comes in in the middle of a meeting, just cover the Apple Watch with your hand to mute it.

Taking a Screenshot

To take a screenshot of your Apple Watch, first make sure that the feature is enabled in the Apple Watch app on your iPhone. Tap General from the Watch app's main screen, then scroll down and tap Enable Screenshots.

With the feature enabled, to take a screenshot, you press the Digital Crown and the Side Button at the same time (or hold the Digital Crown and then press the Side Button). Screenshots are stored in the Camera Roll on your iPhone.

Send a Friend Your Location

It's easy to let someone know where you are using the Messages app on your Watch.

• Open a conversation in Messages.

• Force Touch the screen and tap Send Location.

Reading and Responding to Messages

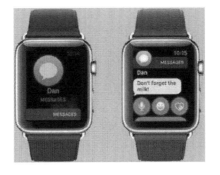

To read a new message, raise your wrist after reading a notification. To dismiss the message, lower your arm.

Sending a New Text Message

Open the Apple Watch's Messages app. Its icon is identical to the one on your iPhone. Then Force Touch the screen and then tap New Message.

Deleting Email

Here's how to get rid of an email directly from your watch.

- Open the Mail app on your Apple Watch.

- Swipe left on any email.

- Tap Trash to delete the message.

Clearing Your Notifications

Notifications piling up? Here's how to dismiss them.

- From the watch face, swipe down from the top of the screen to display your notifications.

- Force Touch the display, then tap Clear All.

Setting Focus and Exposure in the Camera App

The camera on your Apple Watch lets you use the watch as a remote for your iPhone camera. Launch the app, and tap anywhere on the preview image on your Watch to set the focus and exposure.

Ending or Pausing Your Workout

- With a workout in progress, open the Workout app.

- Swipe right on the display.

- Tap End or Pause.

Deleting Apps from Your Apple Watch

- Removing an app from your Apple Watch works much the same way it does on an iPhone.

- From the watch face or any app, press the Digital Crown to go to the Watch's home screen.

- Tap and hold any app icon.

- Tap the small X that appears on any third-party app icon to remove the app from your Watch.

- Tap Delete App to confirm.

Changing Audio Sources

Here's how to control the device — your phone or your watch — from which you play music.

- In the Music app, Force Touch the display, then tap Source.
- Select iPhone to play music from your phone. Select Apple Watch to play music from your watch on a Bluetooth speaker or headphones.

Switching Views in Calendar

- Open the Calendar app, select a day, and then Force Touch the display.
- Select List to see a list of upcoming events or Up Next to see cards of upcoming events. Tap Today to jump to the current day in either view.

Have Mickey/Minnie Mouse Speak the Time

Among the Apple Watch's many faces are two different versions featuring either Mickey or Minnie Mouse. And they can pull off a little trick

- Switch to the Mickey/Minnie Mouse watch face.

- Tap the screen and whichever character you have selected will announce the current time. (You can disable this under Sounds & Haptics in either the Watch's Settings app or the Watch app on your iPhone.)

Activating Siri

To pull up Siri for voice commands, press and hold the Digital Crown. Alternatively, raise your wrist and say "Hey Siri."

Find Your Phone

Your phone is always a quick tap away when you're wearing an Apple Watch.

- From the watch face, swipe up on the display to bring up Control Center.
- Tap the Find Phone icon in the right. Your iPhone will play a sound.

Unpairing Your Apple Watch

If you're upgrading your iPhone, you'll want to make sure you unpair your Apple Watch.

- Open the Apple Watch app on your iPhone, and select your Apple Watch from the main menu.
- On the next screen, tap the "i" button next to your Watch.
- Tap Unpair Apple Watch. (Note that this will back up all settings from your Apple Watch onto your iPhone and then erase your Apple Watch.)

Call Emergency Services

Emergency   SOS was   added   in 2016's
watchOS 3 update.

- Press and hold the Apple Watch's Side
  Button; the power off menu will appear,
  but continue to hold the Side Button
  until the SOS countdown appears.
  (Alternatively, instead of holding the
  Side Button, you can just slide the
  Emergency SOS control on the power
  off   menu.)
- At the end of the countdown, your
  local Emergency Services will be called.
  (Release the button before the end of

the countdown to cancel the call.)

• After the call, your emergency contacts — as set in the Health app on your iPhone — will automatically be notified, and if Location Services on your Watch is off, it will be temporarily activated.

Top 10 Hidden Force Touch Features on Apple Watch

Force Touch is one of those Apple Watch features that's so discreet and unassuming it's easy for users to forget it even exists. That's a shame, because just like 3D Touch on iPhone, Apple has implemented the haptic feedback technology across the entire watchOS interface, putting additional hidden functionality right at your fingertips.

In this section of the book, we've collected 10 of our favorite Force Touch features that work on Apple's digital timepiece. Some are better known than others, but hopefully you'll learn at least one thing new about what a firm press on

your Apple Watch screen can do.

1. Clear All Notifications

The Apple Watch's notifications dropdown can

get busy pretty quickly, especially if you often

forget to dismiss an incoming alert after reading

it. Rather than deleting notifications one by one,

you can clear all of them with a Force Touch

gesture. Simply press firmly on the Notifications

panel and tap the Clear All option.

2. Create and Remove Watch Faces

To create a custom watch face with a background picture, open the Apple Watch Photos app and select a photo. Next, press firmly on the display, tap the Create Watch Face option that pops up, and then select the Photos Face. Alternatively, you can select Kaleidoscope Face to make the picture the basis of a new animating Kaleidoscope.

When you're done, return to the current active watch face and swipe left or right to find your new creation. If you later decide you don't like your new watch face, press down on it to enter Customize Mode, and swipe up on the offending item to delete.

3. Compose a New Message

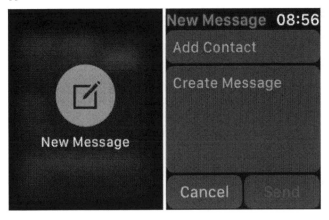

Opening the Mail and Messages apps, you'd be forgiven for thinking the Apple Watch only supports replies. That's because the option to compose a new message is revealed with a Force Touch gesture: Press firmly on the display and tap the New Message button that appears.

You'll now be able to choose a recipient from your Contacts, input a subject if it's an email you're sending, and write your message using dictation, a scribble, or a short pre-defined phrase. Tap send when you're done.

4. Change Move Goal and Get a Weekly Activity Summary

Press down on the Activity screen to reveal a Weekly Summary option that shows how many times you've beaten your daily move goal so far this week.

If you're beating your move goal far too easily – or if you need a little help closing that long red ring on a daily basis – press down on the Activity screen again and tap the Change Move Goal button to adjust the amount of calories you're aiming to burn.

5. Stream Music to an AirPlay Device

If you store music on your Apple Watch, you probably listen to it over connected Bluetooth headphones. But did you know it's also possible to stream it to any audio device that supports AirPlay?

Next time you're on the Music app's Now Playing screen, press firmly on the display and tap the AirPlay button that appears. Choose a nearby AirPlay-supporting device from the list, and you're good to go.

6. Share Your Location With a Contact

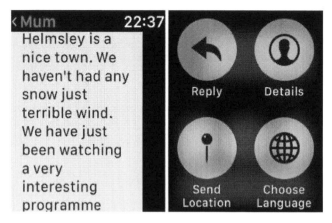

To quickly send your location to someone in an iMessage, open the Messages app on your Apple Watch, select an existing conversation, and activate Force Touch by pressing firmly on the screen. Then simply select the Share Location option from the menu options that appear.

If you haven't enabled it already, you'll be asked to let Messages access your location while using the app (allow it to, otherwise this feature won't work).

7. Switch Map View and Search Local Amenities

Whenever you're looking at a map in the stock Maps app, don't forget that you can change to the Transit/Public Transport view at any time with a simple Force Touch. The same action will also bring up the Search Here option, which lets you dictate or scribble a search term or look up local amenities by selecting from the Food, Shopping, Fun, and Travel submenus.

8. Switch App Screen to List View

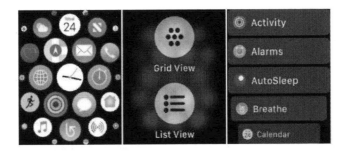

To re-arrange Apple Watch apps in the standard Grid layout, long press the app in question and drag it to where you want it. If you still can't get on with the default Grid view, press down firmly on the screen and try the List view instead.

9. Hourly Temperature Forecast and Chance of Rain

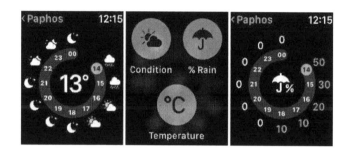

The standard forecast display on the Apple Watch's stock Weather app shows the general weather conditions for the day ahead. But there are two more forecasts available to you. A firm press on the same screen will let you check either the likelihood of rain or any changes in temperature over the next 12 hours.

10. Control Camera Settings Remotely

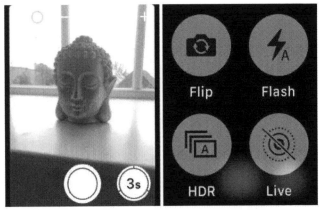

It's not just the shutter of your iPhone's camera that you can remotely control from your wrist. With the Apple Watch Camera app open, press firmly on the screen to reveal a hidden submenu offering access to your iPhone's HDR, Flash, Live Photo, and Flip controls.

How to Control Apple TV Using Your Apple Watch

The Siri Remote that comes with the Apple TV certainly has its critics. Some users find the glass Touch surface over-sensitive in the way it registers directional taps and swipes, which can make navigating onscreen menus a slalo m-like experience where you constantly have to correct for overshoot.

Not only that, the minimalist design of the Siri Remote isn't very tactile and there's no button backlighting, which means once you've dimmed the lights it's almost impossible to know whether you're even holding it the right way round.

Thankfully, there are alternative (and easier) ways to control your Apple TV. One solution is to use your iPhone, another is to use an Apple Watch. Here's how it's done.

How to Link Your Apple Watch to your Apple TV

The steps below assume your Apple Watch is running watchOS 5 and that your Apple TV has tvOS 12 installed.

Before you start, make sure your Apple TV and Apple Watch are on the same Wi-Fi network. To do this on Apple TV, launch the Settings app and navigate to Network -> Wi-Fi. Similarly on Apple Watch, launch the Settings app and tap Wi-Fi.

- Make sure you're in the same room as your Apple TV, your Apple TV is on, and you can see the screen on your TV output.

- On your Apple Watch, launch the Remote app.

- Tap Add Device.

- On your Apple Watch, enter the passcode that appears on your Apple TV's display.

You should now see the Remote interface for controlling your Apple TV on your Apple Watch screen.

How to Control Apple TV Using Your Apple Watch

- Swipe up, down, left, or right to move through the Apple TV menu.
- Tap to choose the selected item.
- Tap Menu to go back.
- Touch and hold Menu to return to the Home screen.
- Swipe left or right to scrub through media.
- Tap to pause or resume playback.

If you're anything like us, you'll find that swiping your Apple Watch to navigate Apple TV menus is much easier than using the Siri Remote – and you'll be able to see what you're doing in the dark. Just remember that as long as your Apple TV is on, you can return to the remote interface on your Apple Watch at any time simply by launching the Remote app.

Without any doubt, I believe you have learned vital things in this book that will help you to maximize your Apple Watch. This book will be updated as more things are evolving. Thanks for purchasing this book, God bless you!

30177291R00057

Printed in Great
Britain
by Amazon